Dispelling Darkness in Turkey

MW01042321

Mary Lou Serratt

Woman's Missionary Union
Birmingham, Alabama

The photographs in this mission study were donated by photographers who serve God with their gifts. Thank you for all you have given Don Martin and Stephen and Edie Smith.

Photographs on pages 58-60 by Don Martin, Richmond, Virginia.

All other photographs by Stephen Smith Commercial and Portrait Images; 931 S. Kansas; Topeka, Kansas 66612; (785) 354-7153.

Many thanks also go to Mari Jaquith and Yvonne Keefer of Kansas-Nebraska WMU for partnering with us to bring you these wonderful photographs.

Woman's Missionary Union
P.O. Box 830010
Birmingham, AL 35283-0010

2000 by Woman's Missionary Union
All rights reserved. First printing 2000.
Printed in the United States of America.
Woman's Missionary Union and WMU are registered trademarks.

Dewey Decimal Classification: 266.023
Subject Headings: Missions, International Missions

Scriptures in this work indicated by CEV are taken from Contemporary English Version, Copyright 1991 by American Bible Society, New York, NY. Used by permission.

Scriptures in this work indicated by NIV are taken from the Holy Bible, New International Version, Copyright 1973, 1978, 1984 International Bible Society. Used by permission of Zondervan Bible Publishers.

ISBN: 1-56309-496-7

W004127 • 0700 • 12.5M1

266

Christian missions

Evangelistic work

Table of Contents

Dispelling the Darkness in Turkey

"May God be gracious to us and bless us and make his face to shine upon us, that your ways may be known on earth, your salvation among the nations. May the peoples praise you, O God; may all the peoples praise you. May the nations be glad and sing for joy, for you rule the peoples justly and guide the nations of the earth. May the peoples praise you, O God; may all the peoples praise you. Then the land will yield its harvest and God, our God will bless us. God will bless us, and all the ends of the earth will fear him" (Psalm 67 NIV).

Not all darkness is bad. Darkness can be comforting, restful, even healing in certain circumstances; but, this is true only if you are in control of the darkness. Then you can dispel it with the click of a light switch, the lighting of a candle, or the flick of a flashlight.

Without that ability to produce a light source, the darkness is in control of you; it becomes oppressive, or perhaps even life threatening. Spiritual darkness is more oppressive and is the darkness in which we must shine with the light of salvation through Christ in every corner of the world.

Turkey, our focus for this mission study, is a country rich with historical and biblical significance, but it is a country overshadowed by spiritual darkness.

"There are those who dwell in such darkness [that] it is difficult for the light to penetrate, and those who have been blessed and surrounded with so much light that they cannot see the bitter darkness of their souls," says Caroline[1], a young woman who participated in a prayer walk in Turkey.

The theme scripture (Psalm 67) does not dwell on the subject of darkness. It is filled with joy, hope, and praise. For the believer, the very thought of God's love and power calls us to express these fact-based emotions. For when His light shines in us and through us, the darkness doesn't have a chance!

It is not our job to moan about the horror of darkness. No! It is our responsibility to be transmitters of God's light so the entire world will be drawn to our light source. Then the light bearers will reach into all the dark corners of the earth, and God will be exalted. And finally all the nations and all the peoples of those nations will turn to Christ, find salvation, and join the praise and worship celebration!

Chapter 1
A Rich History

"I praise you, Lord, for being my guide. Even in the darkest night, your teachings fill my mind" (Psalm 16:7 CEV).

D id you just look back at the title or table of contents thinking, *History! I thought this was a mission study book!?* Perhaps you don't think of yourself as someone who is very interested in history.

You may be surprised by what you discover as you examine the past of the country we call Turkey. You'll find in it packed with familiar events and references that weave in and out of biblical history. Turkey's history is one of accomplishment and failure, of moments of greatness and times of despair. But in even the dark periods, God has been at work. See if you can trace the movement of God through the history of this nation.

Early Historic Highlights

During biblical times, Turkey was known as Anatolia. Only Jericho was more advanced than Anatolia at this time.[2] Studies indicate that the largest town on earth was Catalhoyuk with 6,000 inhabitants.[3] The people lived in houses which had openings on the roofs and ate wheat, lentils and vegetables. They farmed and hunted.

Fine pottery was a major artistic product. Artifacts left by the early dwellers show life was primarily unchanged until the Bronze Age.

An indigenous group called Hatti lived in the central area of Anatolia during the early Bronze Age.[4] They traded gold and silver to caravans in exchange for tin and textiles, and scholars agree that the Hatti were people of advanced intelligence and craftsmanship.

About 2000 BC the Indo-European Hittites first began establishing villages and towns in Anatolia. They built palaces and temples and became one of the great super powers of the Ancient world. Around this same time Abraham arrived in Palestine.[5]

By 1500 BC the Hittites had created a powerful empire and were great rulers of the Middle East.[6] Then struggles with other nations and peoples began. One result was the first recorded peace agreement between states.[7] This was signed between King Ramses of Egypt and the Hittite King, Moursil. More invasions, more wars, and more rulers followed.

Meanwhile, in another part of the world during this period, called the Bronze Age, Egyptians enslaved the Israelites. This was followed by the Exodus and years of wandering in the wilderness.[8]

In 333 BC Alexander the Great conquered the entire Middle East from Greece to India. His policy was both respectful and tolerant, and his method of ruling helped bring about the unification of the East and West. Hence, Anatolia was integrated into Roman territory in 133 BC.[9]

Excavations have given evidence that during all this unrest, the inhabitants continued to excel in different types and styles of workmanship. It seems a fire of creativity and a thirst for beauty and knowledge was placed in the people of Anatolia, and nothing could extinguish it.

The Roman Age

After the Romans conquered Anatolia, its inhabitants enjoyed a period of relative peace. Of even greater significance was the birth of Christ which would change the history of the world. The New Testament period and the period of Roman rule in Anatolia coincide on a timeline.

In this setting, Christianity began to spread. Sometime between 1–10 AD, Paul was born in Tarsus of Cilicia in Anatolia. He became the leader in spreading Christianity throughout the Greco-Roman world. Both Paul and Barnabas visited many cities in the region. The three missionary journeys to Anatolia and Greece spanned more than ten years.

Paul's **first missionary journey**[10] began at Antioch, the modern Turkish city of Antakya. Much of this ministry centered in the province of Galatia, especially in the cities of the south. These included Antioch, Iconium, Lystra and Derbe. On this trip, both Barnabas and John Mark traveled with Paul.

The **second missionary journey**[11] was an overland trip through Turkey to the port of Troas. Silas was Paul's associate on this venture to spread the message of the light of the world.

The **third missionary journey**[12] was centered in Ephesus.[13] During this time, Paul wrote the letter to the Romans. Furthermore, it was at this time that the gospel probably spread into the seven churches (or cities) mentioned in Revelation.[14]

Scholars date these journeys between AD 46 and 61. On each trip the usual mode of entry was to find the synagogue and share the gospel on the Sabbath day. As you can imagine, this usually caused problems, yet groups of believers were formed in most of the places visited by Paul and his companions. Paul, through the inspiration of the Holy Spirit, composed the letters of instruction to the churches.

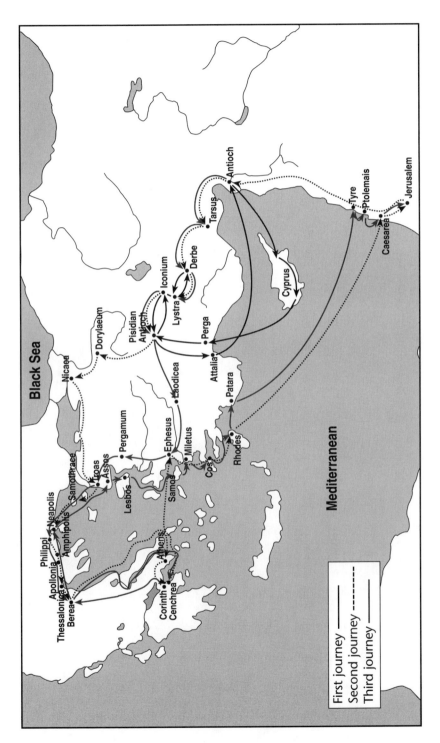

Black Sea

Mediterranean

Antioch
Tarsus
Tyre
Ptolemais
Jerusalem
Caesarea
Cyprus
Derbe
Iconium
Lystra
Pisidian Antioch
Perga
Dorylaeum
Attalia
Laodicea
Patara
Nicaea
Pergamum
Rhodes
Ephesus
Miletus
Cos
Samos
Troas
Assos
Lesbos
Samothrace
Neapolis
Philippi
Amphipolis
Apollonia
Thessalonica
Berea
Athens
Corinth
Cenchrea

First journey ——
Second journey ------
Third journey ——

5

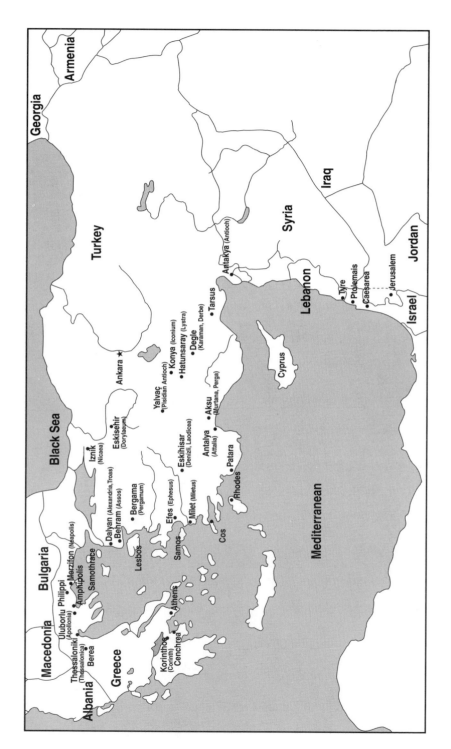

These practical helps to understanding our Christian duty were penned as the soil of Turkey clung to Paul's sandals!

Constantine the Great was the first Roman ruler to become a Christian sometime between 312 and 324 AD. He gradually became more open and involved in his belief. Christianity spread quickly through the cities of the empire.[15]

Three Civilizations

During the Byzantine Period, the Roman Empire was divided into Eastern and Western regions. The Eastern Romans were Christians for the most part, and they changed their language from Latin to Greek. The Byzantine Empire encompassed and ruled the land we now call Turkey until the late 1000's.

In 1071 the Seljuks[16] defeated the Byzantine army and set up an empire. This marked the beginning of the replacement of Christianity and the Greek language with Islam and the Turkish language.

In 1095 Christians in Western Europe began the Crusades, the first military expeditions to the Middle East. Crusade is the Latin word for *cross*. A trail of death, destruction, and ruin resulted, and the Turkish people were impressed with a distorted image of Christ and His church. The purpose of the Crusades was to drive the Turks from the Holy Land. The Seljuk Turks in western Anatolia were defeated and about one third of the country was returned to the Byzantine Empire.

After a brief period of rule by Asian nomads known as Mongols,[17] the influence of the Turks continued to grow in Anatolia.

During the 1300s a group of Turks called the Ottomans[18] began to take over more and more of the land until only Constantinople and the surrounding area remained as the Byzantine Empire.[19] Ottoman forces captured Constantinople in 1453, renaming it Istanbul. The Ottoman Empire reached its height during the reign of Sultan Bayezid II. In later years when Sultan Süleyman the Magnificent began to tire of fighting and withdrew from public responsibilties, various forms of corruption crept into the government. Nepotism and other forms of corruption left the Ottoman Empire in a steady state of decline and weakened the central government.

Dennis R. Papazian, a professor of history at the University of Michigan, described the Ottoman reign: "The Ottoman Empire at its zenith was well governed, and religious and national minorities were treated as well as any place in the known world. With its decline, however, the Empire became a corrupt and backward state. Christians were treated as *gavours* (infidels) and denied basic civil, religious, and human rights; and, at times, they suffered dire persecutions."[20]

Influenced by the ideals of the French Revolution and bowing to pressure from Europe and its own non-Muslim subjects, the Sultans of the Ottoman Empire sought to bring reform to the Empire.[21] One result was the adoption of the first constitution in 1876. It granted people a representative government and other freedoms.

During this period of freedom and tolerance, Armenian Christians in the Empire were able to gain governmental recognition for the Armenian National Constitution, a document which governed the church and community. That same year, Sultan Abdul-Hamid II came into power and set the constitution aside, choosing to be a dictator.

Religious persecution spread. Between 1894 and 1918, many Christian Armenians died because of their beliefs. Various factions of Turkish military became discontented with Abdul-Hamid II's disregard of the constitution and led a revolt which was eventually named the Young Turk Revolution.[22] In 1909, revolutionary forces gained the advantage and the "constitution was amended to transfer real power to the parliament."[23] The Balkan Wars between 1912 and 1913 resulted in the loss of nearly all Ottoman holdings in Europe. During World War I the Ottoman Empire sided with Germany. The Young Turks' government used the war as an opportunity to deal with internal problems. One of these was the Christian Armenian contingent in eastern Asia Minor and Cilicia who were either massacred or forced to flee.[24] In 1918 the Ottoman Empire lost much of its territory because of its alliance with Germany.

The Republic Period

In 1923 the Grand National Assembly proclaimed the Republic of Turkey. The borders set then remain much the same today.

Mustafa Kemal became the first president and chose the city of Ankara as the new capital. He had been a military genius and showed great strength as the country's leader. In 1935 everyone took a surname and Mustafa Kemal received the name Atatürk which means "Father of the Turks."

With the birth of this new nation came sweeping social changes. During Kemal Atatürk's presidency, a constitution was adopted which kept Islam as the state religion. However, in 1928 the constitution was amended, removing Islam as the official religion and leaving Turkey as a secular republic. Nationalism was encouraged. Under Kemal Atatürk, polygamy was abolished, the fez (described by Webster's as "a brimless cone-shaped flat-crowned hat that ususally has a tassel, is usually made of red felt , and is worn especially by men") was prohibited, and women were given the right to vote and serve in parliament. Friday, the Muslim holy day, became a weekday, and Sunday became the official day of rest. The Latin alphabet was introduced. "Peace at home, peace in the world" became the slogan for foreign policy. Atatürk remained in power in Turkey until his death in 1938. He is still considered a hero.

Turkey's Recent Past

When Atatürk died in 1938, Ismet Inönü was elected as president and kept Turkey from entering WWII until 1945 when Germany's defeat was certain. In 1945 Turkey joined the United Nations as one of the original member states. In 1947 the United States gave economic and military aid to help Turkey resist Soviet expansion.

In 1946 the Democrat Party was formed as a spin-off of the Republican People's Party established by Atatürk. Prime Minister Recep Peker and others tried to prevent the formation of this second party, but were overruled by President Inönü.[25] The formation of other political parties soon followed.

In 1950 the Democrat Party defeated the Republican People's Party. Celâl Bayar was elected president, and Adnan Menderes was appointed to the post of prime minister, "a post which for the first time came to surpass that of the president in importance."[26] Turkey entered the Korean War, and changes brought increased national debt and restricted the freedom of speech.

In 1960 the military seized control of the government and imprisoned President Bayar. A new constitution was adopted in 1961.

Also during the 60s Turkey and Greece came close to war over the island of Cyprus. Fighting broke out in Cyprus in 1964 and again in 1967. Turkish forces invaded Cyprus in 1974. The issue of Greek or Turkish control of Cyprus remains a divisive issue to this day with Turkish immigrants occupying the northern third of Cyprus.

Since the 1960s, high taxes, inflation, and radical groups staging terrorist acts have troubled Turkey. Bombings, kidnappings, and murders occured. In the 1970s disputes between secular and religious groups developed. Fighting with the Kurdish[27] rebels in the southeast began in 1984. Free elections in 1983 placed Turgut Oal in power, and his rule led to a business boom lasting until his death in 1993.

Unrest and uncertainty have colored the recent history of Turkey. Problems have almost blotted out the flashes of improvement in the country. Most in the nation would agree there is a need for illumination and clarity of purpose. Many wonder what the future holds.

Turkey Tidbits

The busy port town of Ephesus was a base of operations used by Paul and the early church to carry the gospel throughout the Roman world. The noisy, busy trading center of Asia Minor was a travel center for those going to Greece, Italy, and Rome.

Visitors now view ruins of the 24,000 seat theater where crowds shouted in protest to Paul's message (Acts 19:34). Though there are few Christians today, there are none today proclaiming Diana's greatness!

Atatürk's reforms seem to remain as the basis for life in Turkey today.

Call to Prayer

Claim His promise: "I waited patiently for the Lord; he turned to me and heard my cry. He lifted me out of the slimy pit, out of the mud and mire; he set my feet on a rock and gave me a firm place to stand. He put a new song in my mouth, a hymn of praise to our God. Many will see and fear and put their trust in the Lord" (Psalm 40:1-3 NIV).

- **PRAY** for the millions of people living in the historic city of Istanbul, center of many events through the ages.
- **PRAY** for an open attitude among those who still connect the cross of Jesus Christ with the symbol of the bloody Crusades.
- **PRAY** that Christians from around the world who participated in the Reconciliation Walks of the late 1990s will have a continued influence on those with whom they were in contact.
- **PRAY** for understanding among the different ethnic groups in Turkey who have had a difficult shared history in the land.
- **PRAY** that old family or territorial wounds will be healed in a setting of peace and respect, opening the doors to more ministry opportunities.
- **PRAISE** God for those who will find that firm rock of salvation this year.

The Sultanahmet Mosque in Istanbul; also called the Blue Mosque

Chapter 2
Exploring Turkey 2000

"Let him who walks in the dark, who has no light, trust in the name of the Lord and rely on his God" (Isaiah 50:10b NIV).

When you see the word "Turkey," what comes to your mind? If your answer is Thanksgiving, pilgrims, and cranberry sauce, it is time to do some exploring!

To go exploring, we first need to choose our destination and plot our trip. Look at a map of the Middle East to discover Turkey's location. At once we notice something interesting: Turkey is a nation that occupies both Europe and Asia. About three percent of the people live in the region called Thrace in the tip of southern Europe. Turkey's largest city, Istanbul, is situated amid the lush greenery of this region, but also straddles the Bosphorus strait into the remaining area of the country called Anatolia or Asia Minor. Anatolia sprawls across that mountainous peninsula. Farmland is scattered through this rocky, barren area. This is also home to the capital city of Ankara (population approximately 3.2 million).

Turkey, measuring 483,260 square miles, is approximately the size of Texas. Though small as nations are measured, it continues to maintain an important place in history because of its location. Turkey controls the Bosphorus and Dardanelles, the sea links between the Black Sea and the Mediterranean.

We can enter Turkey from any of the seven countries that share a border: Greece, Bulgaria, Georgia, Armenia, Iran, Iraq, or Syria; or via the Mediterranean, Aegean, or Black Seas. If we choose to fly there, we can land at one of 118 or more airports. Most have paved runways.

Enjoying the Variety

A growing number of people like to visit Turkey because of the great choices available. Enjoy mountains, valleys, rivers, or beaches. Forests are still available along the Mediterranean coast and the Black Sea area. In fact, forests and wooded areas make up 26 percent of the country.

The Eastern Plateau offers both giant mountains and flat plains. The highest point in the nation, Mount Ararat (17,011 feet), is located near the Iranian border. Sound familiar? Read Gen. 8:4,[28] 2 Kings 19:37,[29] Isaiah 37:38, or Jer. 51:27 if you need a reminder of some important events linked to that place.

The Western Valleys along the coast of the Aegean Sea have the richest crops in Turkey, including barley, corn, olives, tobacco, and wheat. Crops of the Southern Plains also include citrus fruits and cotton while farmers on the Northern Plains grow nut crops and use the land for grazing.

Ten Eye Bridge over the Tigress River

The Southeastern part of the country is home to most of the nation's Kurds. They raise cotton, tobacco, and sugar beets, and herd goats and sheep.

Another variable in Turkey is the climate. Thrace and the south and west coasts of Anatolia have hot, dry summers and cool, wet winters. In Northeastern Turkey the summers are mild, but the winters are very cold with temperatures sometimes dropping to –40 F. Heavy snowstorms are common in Southeastern Turkey and the interior of the country.

The greatest natural disasters are earthquakes, primarily occuring in northern Turkey. In recent times these have drawn the attention of the world to focus on this country.

If you aren't interested in hiking the 620 miles from the Black Sea to the Mediterranean or observing the bears, wild boars, and leopards that share the country with the Turks, you have other options.

Places to Visit

You already know to take a history book and a Bible with you to visit the attractions in Turkey. Exploring Turkey is best done with a sense of adventure and a pair of comfortable walking shoes!

A good place to start is Istanbul[30], the capital of the civilized world for many centuries. It is divided into three sections by waterways. Now it is home to 12 million people. Istanbul is a study in contrasts. Standing on a street corner, you might find a McDonald's and a mosque in the same line of vision. You won't find many super markets, but there is a grocery store on each corner and a variety of goods at the open-air markets. Hagia Sophia, the Church of the Divine Wisdom, was built here 14 centuries ago. This cathedral, now a mosque, is a prime example of Byzantine architecture and was once called the greatest church in Christendom.

Another city of interest is the capital. Ankara[31] is located in the desert of Central Anatolia. The presidential mansion used by Atatürk is a reminder of the love and respect he was given. You will be reminded of this as you see statues and monuments dedicated to him throughout the country. Roman ruins are mingled with the Muslim mosques in Ankara today.

In southeastern Anatolia, crumbling walls and ruined buildings lead to Harran (modern spelling of the biblical city of Haran), one of the earth's oldest cities. Abraham was an early inhabitant (Gen. 11:31). It was in Harran that God gave him a call to migrate to Canaan and told him the future held a great honor. The stars Abraham gazed on still light the night sky. Some residents of Harran continue to live in beehive-shaped, mud houses.

Do you always save dessert for last? Then you will be happy with the final city on our tour. Ephesus[32] is one of Turkeys' grandest and most well-preserved ancient cities. It was once a center of politics, religion, and commerce. It was a hub for the ministries of Paul,[33] Timothy,[34] and the apostle John.[35] Ephesus and its people are mentioned at least 20 times in the New Testament. The city was known for its wealth and beauty. The Temple of Diana was counted as one of the Seven Wonders of the World. At the time of Paul's visits, Ephesus had a population of about 250,000, making it the fourth largest city in the world. The church was founded on his second missionary journey.[36] On his third journey[37] Paul returned there and stayed for over two years. The Turkish town of Selçuk occupies the site of the ancient city. Today we may share Paul's same greeting to the people in the cities of Turkey: "Grace and peace to you from God our Father and the Lord Jesus Christ!" (Ephesians 1:2 NIV)

15

The Economic Picture

The Turkish economy is brighter today than in the past. In 1997 inflation was 99 percent; in 1998 it had declined to about 70 percent. That is good news for the people. The growing economy is a mix of the modern and traditional.

Major industries include motor vehicles, petroleum, engineering, and tourism while the largest exports are textiles and clothing. Most factories and mills are located in urban areas of northern and western Turkey.

Turkey is rich in minerals, including coal, chromite, copper, bauxite, and iron ore.

In most years Turkey produces enough food for their country with some to export. Over 40 percent of the people are involved in agriculture. About half the farmland is used for producing grains, including wheat, barley, and corn. Tobacco is a major export, and wool is the primary livestock product.

The industrial production growth rate in 1998 was 4.1 percent, and the unemployment rate for the same year was 10 percent.

Government

Turkey has a republican parliamentary democracy with a constitution which was adopted in 1982. The constitution provides for a president, a prime minister and cabinet, and a legislature called the Grand National Assembly.

The chief of state (president) is elected by the National Assembly for a seven-year term. President Ahmet Necdet Sezer was elected in May 5, 2000. The president is the commander in chief of armed forces and presides at cabinet meetings.

The prime minister is Turkey's head of government, selected by the president. Prime Minister Bulent Evevit was appointed in 1999.

Forming the legislative branch, the Grand National Assembly has the power by the Constitution to make laws, ratify treaties, and declare war. These 550 members are elected by popular vote and serve five-year terms.

Turkey is made up of provinces, each with an appointed governor.

Current problems in Turkey include human rights violations, corruption, an unstable economy, and ethnic struggles with the Kurds. Roughly ten million Kurds populate the country. The arrest of the Kurdish leader of the PKK (Worker's Party of Kurdistan), Abdullah Ocalan, in February of 1999 accelerated the problem.

Turkey seems always to be in the world's spotlight. Decisions made in the coming months could have an impact beyond the nation's boundaries.

Turkey Tidbits

Population: 67 million[38]
Life expectancy: 73.29 years
Ethnic groups: Turkish (75-85%); Kurdish (14-19%)
Languages: Turkish (90%), Kurdish (7%), Arabic (1%),
            plus some Greek, Armenian, and Yiddish
Literacy: 82.3% can read and write
Voting age: 18 years
Flag: red with white crescent and star
Labor force: 22.7 million[39]
Currency: Turkish lira
Telephones: 17 million[40]

Call to Prayer

Claim His promise: "In the same way, the Spirit helps us in our weakness. We do not know what we ought to pray for, but the Spirit himself intercedes for us with groans that words cannot express. And he who searches our hearts knows the mind of the Spirit, because the Spirit intercedes for the saints in accordance with God's will" (Romans 8:26,27 NIV).

PRAY for government leaders to be open and responsive to hearing the truth of His word.

PRAY for continued freedom to inquire about the Christian faith and for increased recognition of this freedom by individuals.

PRAY for openness among the Kurdish population to hear the message of God's unconditional love and to understand His promise of true peace.

PRAY for those living in the remote mountainous areas of the country to have access to hear the gospel and to identify with the Christ who was at home in villages and gave parables about crops and sheep.

PRAY for those who make their living along the coast and rivers through the fishing industry to hear the message of why people were called to become fishers of men.

PRAY for the people living in Selçuk to develop an interest in the ruins they walk among daily and the message of the person called Paul who lived there.

PRAISE God for putting into our hearts and minds His desires for the people in Turkey as we lift them to God in prayer.

Chapter 3
Understanding the People

"The light shines in the darkness, but the darkness has not understood it" (John 1:5 NIV).

The greatest resource of any nation is its people. Knowing facts about where they live and the work they do doesn't necessarily help us understand how they feel or what their dreams are. To understand the people of any country, we need to learn about their religion and their culture—and in Turkey these two aspects are often intermingled.

Religion
99.5 percent of the people living in Turkey are Muslim. Christians and Jews comprise only 0.2 percent of the population. Turkey has no state religion and religious freedom is a guarantee, according to the constitution.

Islam
The word *Islam* in Arabic is literally translated "Way of Submission (or Surrender)." Islam is based on the writings of the Al Qur'an or Koran, which Muslims consider to be the holy scriptures of God (Allah). These scriptures were revealed through the prophet Mohammed in the Arabic language and are not to be translated. They are translated in many languages for the sake of the common man's understanding, but they are recited, memorized, and repeated in prayer rituals in Arabic.

Muslims follow the teaching of prophets through whom they believe God has revealed himself since the dawn of time. Many of those considered to be prophets in Islam are found in the Old Testament such as Adam, Noah, Abraham, David, Solomon, etc. Jesus is the prophet preceding Mohammed. Although they believe and the Qur'an states that Jesus was born of the Virgin Mary, that an angel appeared to Mary and announced his coming birth, and that Jesus performed miracles; they do not believe him to be God incarnate in human form, nor do they believe he was crucified and raised from the dead to provide salvation to all people.

19

"Behold!" the Angel said, God has chosen you, and puri-
fied you, and chosen you above the women of all nations.
Mary, God gives you good news of a word from Him,
whose name shall be the Messiah, Jesus son of Mary, honored in this world and in the Hereafter, and one of those
brought near to God. He shall speak to the people from
his cradle and in maturity, and he shall be of the right-
eous. She said: "My Lord! How shall I have a son when no
man has touched me?' He said: "Even so; God creates
what He will. When He decrees a thing, He says to it, 'Be!'
and it is" (Sura 3:42-47).

The Qur'an also refers to Jesus being raised up to heaven by God,
and it does say that He will be present on the day of judgement:

And there is not one of the followers of the Book but most
certainly believes in this before his death, and on the day
of resurrections he (Jesus) shall be a witness against them
(Sura 4:159).

Mohammed was born in Saudi Arabia in the city of Mecca about 572
AD. He was born into a poor family but married a rich widow when
he was a young man. Because he didn't need to work, he had time
to think about deep subjects, including religion. Although Judaism
and Christianity had arrived in Saudi Arabia, most people there still
worshiped idols.

Each year Mohammed would go to Mt. Hira to think and pray.
One year when he returned, he announced he had experienced a
vision and he declared himself a chosen prophet of Allah, or God.

For nine years he preached his messages and gained followers. In
612 these followers persuaded him to leave Mecca because of threats
made on his life. He continued to gather followers and returned to
the city in victory in 630 AD. At that time he was acknowledged as
"the prophet," or greatest prophet, by all the country.

The followers of Mohammed recorded all his messages and visions
since he could not write. About ten years after his death, these were
collected and became the Qur'an, or the Holy Book of Islam. It has
114 chapters and 6236 verses.

The Qur'an is greatly revered by all Muslims and treated as a holy
object. Many Christians mistakenly view Mohammed as the Islamic
parallel to our Christian worship of Christ. However, the Al Qur'an is
considered a holy revelation from Allah and an incarnation.
Mohammed is not considered divine, nor is he worshiped. Thus, a
better understanding of Islam would be this parallel:

The Al Qur'an is to Muslims as Jesus Christ is to Christians.

an open Qur'an

The death of the prophet created a problem. The followers did not expect another prophet, for Mohammed was the *Seal of the Prophets.* However, they needed a leader to ensure the continued growth of the Islamic religion.

One of the first converts to Islam and a friend of Mohammed, Abu Bakr, was elected. His title was *Successor to the Messenger of God.*[41] From the beginning the leader was recognized over both religion and state. Islam was considered a complete system for the socio-political, moral, and spiritual government. During the early stages of Islam, doctrine was established concentrating on the issues of faith and works, predestination, revelation, the eternal nature of the Qur'an, and the literal interpretation of it. These early followers of Abu Bakr and the established doctrine were the Sunni, or conservative Muslims, and are still the predominant group in the world today.

At the time of Mohammed's death, another group of followers believed Mohammed's first cousin and son-in-law, Ali b Abi Talib, was the better person to lead the faith. This group, known as Shi'at Ali, later became known as Shi'a Muslims. They believed in the appointment of successors, called imams, and felt Mohammed had appointed Ali.

The most important difference between the two groups concerns the authority of the Qur'an. The Sunni believe the Qur'an is the final word and there is no later revelation. The Shi'a believe that the imam has both divine inspiration and the authority of Allah to add to the Qur'an; they are considered to be more radical than the Sunni.

Through the years, other groups of Islam have developed, including the Druze who believe Ali was an incarnation of God and the Ismaelis who became active missionaries, spreading Islam to southern Arabia and East Africa.

Many Turks also practice folk Islam, claiming charms offer protection from evil. Another sect, the Sufi brotherhoods, pursue mystical forms of Islam. They are also known as "Tarikat" in Turkey.

21

The Five Pillars of Islam

The five pillars are a guide for the religious practices of Muslims. Each is commanded in the Al Qur'an, and most Muslims believe they are fulfilling their religious duties by regularly committing to these practices. The frequency of which these commands are followed often depend on the society, culture, and individual religious devotion. Some in Turkey are very devoted to the five pillars while others pursue a more secular life and only commit to the five pillars on religious holidays.

1. *Confess that there is no God but Allah and Mohammed is his prophet (Shahadah or Kalimah).* Muslims believe there is only one true creator God (Allah). All forms of idolatry are strictly forbidden. Thus, the Christian concept of the Trinity is difficult to understand and problematic for Muslims. Many may mistakenly believe Christians worship three gods (God, Jesus Christ, and the Holy Spirit).

> O followers of the Book! do not exceed the limits in your religion, and do not speak (lies) against Allah, but (speak) the truth; the Messiah, Jesus son of Mary is only an apostle of Allah and His Word which He communicated to Mary and a spirit from Him; believe therefore in Allah and His apostles, and say not, Three. Desist, it is better for you; Allah is only one God; far be It from His glory that He should have a son, whatever is in the heavens and whatever is in the earth is His, and Allah is sufficient for a Protector (Sura 4:171).

Muslims must believe and declare faith by making this confession.

2. *Prayer (Salah).* Muslims must pray five times a day: sunrise (Fajr), midday (Dhuhr), mid afternoon ('Asr), sunset (Maghrib), and night (Isha'). Muslims must go through a ritual washing of the head, hands, and feet and cover themselves before praying. Shoes must be removed. One may pray individually or with others, at home, in a prayer room or at the mosque. Pray-ers face towards Mecca and kneel, stand and bow on a prayer rug. There are prescribed prayers, confessions (in Arabic), and positions, plus an optional time to pray additional prayers to God (in one's own language). The day of worship is on Friday at noon (Jum'ah) when Muslims go to the mosque to pray. This is usually accompanied by a sermon. The educated Muslim leader is called the imam.

And certainly Allah made a covenant with the children of

Israel, and We raised up among them twelve chieftains; and Allah said: Surely I am with you; if you keep up prayer and pay the poor-rate and believe in My apostles and assist them and offer to Allah a goodly gift, I will most certainly cover your evil deeds, and I will most certainly cause you to enter into gardens beneath which rivers flow, but whoever disbelieves from among you after that, he indeed shall lose the right way. (Sura 5:12)

3. *Fasting (Sawm)*. During the month of Ramadan[42] (on the ninth month of the lunar calendar) all Muslims except those with special exemptions should fast from sunup to sundown. They should fast from all food and drink, medicines, smoking, sexual relations, lying, gossip, and quarreling. At the end of the day, they should break the fast with prayer and food or drink. Additional prayers are usually done during this time, and many go to the mosque at night to recite the Qur'an. At the end of the month the fasting is ended with a day of celebration and feasting: Id al'Fitr.[43] Most wake early and go to the mosque to pray, then visit family and friends, eating and asking forgiveness of others for their sins of the past year. Many Muslims believe their spirits are cleansed by fasting and begging forgiveness.

The month of Ramadan is that in which the Qur'an was revealed, a guidance to men and clear proofs of the guidance and the distinction; therefore whoever of you is present in the month, he shall fast therein, and whoever is sick or upon a journey, then (he shall fast) a (like) number of other days; Allah desires ease for you, and He does not desire for you difficulty, and (He desires) that you should complete the number and that you should exalt the greatness of Allah for His having guided you and that you may give thanks. (Sura 2:185)

4. *Alms to the poor (Zakah)*. A tax upon one's belongings is required by Islamic law, which is given to the poor. Many believe that sharing their wealth with others, like fasting, is an act of purification.

If you give alms openly, it is well, and if you hide it and give it to the poor, it is better for you; and this will do away with some of your evil deeds; and Allah is aware of what you do (Sura 2:271).

5. *Pilgrimage to Mecca (Hajj)*. A pilgrimage to Mecca is required of every Muslim man and woman at least once in his or her lifetime,

provided he or she has the means to do so. Pilgrims on the Hajj perform specific rituals, visit certain places, and wear unsewn white garments. At the end of the journey there is a special day of feasting, prayer, and animal sacrifice called Id al-Adha.[44] Muslims believe that all who go on the Hajj will go to Paradise when they die.

> And accomplish the pilgrimage and the visit for Allah, but if, you are prevented, (send) whatever offering is easy to obtain, and do not shave your heads until the offering reaches its destination; but whoever among you is sick or has an ailment of the head, he (should effect) a compensation by fasting or alms or sacrificing, then when you are secure, whoever profits by combining the visit with the pilgrimage (should take) what offering is easy to obtain; but he who cannot find (any offering) should fast for three days during the pilgrimage and for seven days when you return; these (make) ten (days) complete; this is for him whose family is not present in the Sacred Mosque, and be careful (of your duty) to Allah, and know that Allah is severe in requiting (evil). The pilgrimage is (performed in) the well-known months; so whoever determines the performance of the pilgrimage therein, there shall be no intercourse nor fornication nor quarrelling amongst one another; and whatever good you do, Allah knows it; and make provision, for surely the provision is the guarding of oneself, and be careful (of your duty) to Me, O men of understanding (Sura 2:196-197).

The Qur'an actually speaks of four holy books of Islam: the Taurat, Zabur, Injeel, and Qur'an. The Taurat are the first five books of the Old Testament, the Zabur are the writings of David and Solomon, and the Injeel are the gospels. However, it is believed that these first three books were corrupted over time and through translation. Muslims believe Jews and Christians are reading corrupted versions of scripture and not God's true word. Hence, most Muslims only study the Qur'an.

> And if they had kept up the Taurat and the Injeel and that which was revealed to them from their Lord, they would certainly have eaten from above them and from beneath their feet there is a party of them keeping to the moderate course, and (as for) most of them, evil is that which they do (Sura 5:66).

24

Muslims believe God is the Creator of the world and humankind. They believe their salvation depends on the number of good deeds they have done to outweigh the bad as well as their faith (seen through confession). To become a Muslim, one must confess that there is no God but Allah and Mohammed is his prophet. Muslims believe in a Hell and a Paradise and that God ultimately makes the decision whether an individual is worthy of entering Paradise. There is no assurance of salvation. They must trust in Allah's will without questioning it, and they have little concept of God's forgiveness and mercy (what we know through Jesus) or the actuality of a personal relationship with God.

> And as to those who believe and do good deeds, He will pay them fully their rewards; and Allah does not love the unjust (Sura 3:57).

> And the measuring out on that day will be just; then as for him whose measure (of good deeds) is heavy, those are they who shall be successful; And as for him whose measure (of good deeds) is light those are they who have made their souls suffer loss because they disbelieved in Our communications (Sura 7:8-9).

The Qur'an is a book that teaches both peace and war. Christians and Jews are referred to as "People of the Book" (Ahl al-Kitab), and Muslims are commanded to be tolerant of their religious cousins. On the other hand, the Qur'an also makes reference to holy war (Jihad). Muslims who die in holy wars for the purpose of securing the freedom to practice their religion are thought to go straight to Paradise.[45]

Other sayings of Mohammed and stories of his life can be found in the Hadith. These books are not considered divine, as is the Qur'an; but they are used in understanding and putting into practice the scriptures of the Qur'an.

Christianity

From history and the Bible, you know the rich Christian heritage in Turkey. It was the first nation to officially become Christian in the 4th century AD. However, since the beginning of Islam, very few have chosen to follow Jesus.

Today the New Testament is available in the modern Turkish language. The Old Testament, presently available only in an older Turkish dialect, is currently being translated into modern Turkish.

Customs and Culture

Webster's Dictionary defines culture as "the integrated pattern of human knowledge, belief, and behavior that depends upon man's capacity for learning and transmitting knowledge to succeeding generations."

Culture is what makes it great to wrap a birthday present in cheery red paper for someone in your family but inappropriate to do the same for a Japanese friend. It is why "Yes, sir" is missing from the vocabulary of most ten-year-olds, but sounds like music to the 60-year-old ears! Culture is why "on time" is something to be discussed if you are planning a meeting with someone from a different background. Otherwise, your "on time" may be either very early or very late! In any discussion of culture, I always quote a friend: "This is always true unless it's not."

Perhaps the best way to understand the people is to ask some questions concerning their customs and culture.

What are the people of Turkey like? It is easy to make generalizations about the people of any nation, but this does not give us a true picture. If someone said to you, "Tell me the ten major characteristics of American people," you would think it an impossible task! You would want to ask, "Do you mean those in the North or the South, those under 20 years of age or those over 50, those who have material wealth or the homeless?" And the categories would go on and on! I read recently that butterfly eyes are made up of hun-

man knitting head coverings

dreds of lenses, each angled at different positions. They see things from literally hundreds of perspectives. Sometimes we see only what is most obvious. To understand the people of Turkey, we need butterfly eyes!

If one word had to be chosen to describe the Turks, it would be unique. It is hard to connect them with any other country. The Turks' origin was in the deserts of Asia. They have been influenced by one thousand years of Islam and six centuries of being part in and part out of Europe. They seem to have little in common with the Arabs of the Middle East but share some similarities with both Asians and Europeans.

Two famous quotes from Atatürk are helpful in understanding these interesting people:

He's a lucky man who can say "I am a Turk."

So what does it matter if our regime does not resemble democracy, does not resemble socialism, does not resemble anything? Gentlemen, we should be proud of not resembling anything; because we resemble ourselves, gentlemen!

Turks are unique. Among other things, they are unique because they have migrated from one part of the world to another and changed their script from Runic to Sogdian to Arabic and to Roman.

Some distinctive character traits of Turks might include:
1. *They place great value on honor.* The most shameful of all crimes in Turkey is not murder, but theft. Trust is very important, and this is even extended to the visitor. An English traveler tells about being in a taxi without enough money to pay his fare. The driver said it was no problem; it could be paid later . . . then he did not even ask for the Englishman's name or address! Can you imagine that happening in New York, San Francisco, or even your own city?
2. *The Turks are very sensitive.* They show great understanding, courtesy, and humanity. They are very careful not to hurt another person's feelings. Compare the following proverbs:

United States: Sticks and stones may break my bones, but words will never hurt me.

Turkey: The hurt of a stick dies away, but words hurt forever.

3. *The Turks are contemplative.* Long periods of time can be spent listening to music which is often quite sad. Another favorite pasttime is daydreaming. We might consider this a melancholy personality in our society or perceive it as indifference or apathy.
4. *The Turks have a great pride in their nation.* Their beloved leader, Atatürk, told them: "Be proud, work hard, be confident." It seems most Turks follow those dictates in that order today.
5. *The Turks have retained many oriental virtues.* Among these are the importance of courtesy and hospitality, gift giving, and an aversion to hurry and worry. Is it any wonder American tourists are enchanted with the country?

The majority of visitors to Turkey come away with a picture of the people as kind, helpful, and sincere.

Relationships

How Turks interact with one another helps us understand the Turkish culture. Let's look at relationships, recognizing that some differences of custom will occur based on such variables as working and living conditions. Villagers generally hold on to tradition, are more conservative, and are less likely to be influenced by the West.

bookstore owner and family

Family (Traditional)

Family is very important in Turkey. Parental respect is momentous. The oldest male in the family is the prime authority figure. Others, even grown sons, will not be disrespectful in any way. This includes not smoking, drinking, or even speaking to others in his presence. In the home, the responsibilities of meal preparation, childcare, and housework belong to the woman. The children help parents with the work and attend school. In some instances, marriages are arranged, and in most instances, parental approval is requested.

Friends

Friendship, or *arkadaslik*, is a very strong factor in Turkey. A man's most important bond is with other men. On the street, you see men walking together hand in hand or rushing to greet each other with an embrace. Friendship is something to be treasured and depended on. In this environment, the word *friend* is not used lightly. We can surmise that women also have strong friendship ties, but they are not as evident because women generally do not lead very public lives.

aquaducts in Istanbul (top left)

conservative Muslim (top right)

washing feet before entering mosque (left)

the Sultanahmet Mosque (or Blue Mosque) in Istanbul at dusk (bottom)

semi-conservatively dressed Muslim women (left)

inside the Hagia Sophia mosque (middle left)

conservatively dressed Muslim woman on the streets of Istanbul (middle right)

mosaic in Hagia Sophia, which was once a cathedral (bottom)

the University of Istanbul (right)

feeding the birds in the university courtyard (bottom left)

courtyard of a mosque (bottom right)

the call to prayer has been issued (top)

the Hagia Sophia mosque (left)

horse resting as gypsy boys play near crumbling wall in Fatih, an area of Istanbul (bottom left)

mosque and Istanbul traffic (bottom right)

young men in Diyarbakir (right)

many modes of transportation—walking, train, motorcycle (middle)

poster with a drawing of Kemal Atatürk (bottom left)

boy from the Fatih orphanage (bottom right)

young couple (left)

social gathering courtyard for men only (middle)

produce vendor in Ortakoy (bottom left)

young man relaxing in a park (bottom right)

government building in Istanbul (top)

soccer stadium in Taksim (right)

McDonald's in front of the Ortakoy Cami mosque (bottom left)

trash hauler in Taksim (bottom right)

back terrace of Ciragan Palace (top)

a harbor in Istanbul (middle)

Turkish bath house (bottom left)

looking out from the library of Celsus in Ephesus
(bottom right)

the amphitheater where Paul preached in Ephesus (top)

original entrance to the amphitheater (right)

view of the ruins at Ephesus and of Ayasuluk Castle (bottom)

fish market at Besiktas (top)
Men fishing on the Bosphorus (middle)
the Aegean Sea (bottom)

It's a market under the tents! Under miles of sheet-like tents, shoppers find everything they need . . .

. . . fruits and vegetables . . .

. . . flowers . . .

. . . spices . . .

. . . bread . . .

entrance to St. John's Basilica (top)

bath house at Ephesus (right)

exterior of Mary's House (bottom)

greenhouses outside of Izmir (top)
wedding party (middle left)

dressed for a wedding (middle right)
men selling prayer beads (bottom)

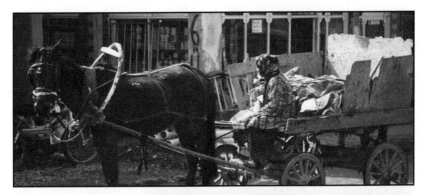

woman uses an older mode of travel in Golcük (top)

woman retrieving raw silk at a carpet weaving school (middle)

vegetable stands in a tent bazaar (bottom left)

outdoor carnival (bottom center)

Kemal Atatürk is still revered throughout the land (bottom right)

Business

Business relationships are built on honor and pride. Even in business, Turks often seem to express that money is not to be discussed or to be regarded as too important. In 1923 the Turks began the transition into a modern commercial and technical society. This has been one of their greatest challenges, because many of the minority groups who had done this type of work left the country around this time. Today many Turks stand out in the fields of business and industry.

Women

The role of women in Turkey is a changing and sometimes contradictory picture. Much of this is due to the Islamic perspective on women.[46] Yet since the formation of the Republic of Turkey, women have had a more active role in this male-dominated society. During World War II, they entered the workforce as teachers, clerical workers, and industrial laborers. Today, many serve as judges, writers, and journalists. They are outstanding contributors in many areas of the arts, including drama, dance, and music. Before the 1920's, Turkish women had almost no rights.

Activities

The activities which Turkish people are engaged in are also lessons in culture. The role of Islam in Turkish society and politics continues to be an issue of debate.

Work

This is one area of great variety. In the cities, many Turkish men and women enjoy professional careers as doctors, lawyers, architects, and engineers. For the majority of the population who live in villages, farming, and raising livestock are a way of life. Some rural dwellers still live as nomads, moving their sheep and their tents to greener pastures. In 1996 employment was divided into these categories: agriculture 42.5 percent, services 34.5 percent, and industry 23 percent.

traditional and modern styles together

Education

Education is available and encouraged. Only in remote villages is there a problem because of rising costs and lack of teachers. After graduation from primary school students may attend middle school.

They must then decide to enter a college preparatory school, vocational school, or the work force. There are more than 25 universities in the country.

Diet

Eating is one activity we can all relate to! You know already about the crops grown in Turkey. Cracked wheat bread and yogurt are part of the main diet. Turks also consume vegetables, olives, fresh fruits, nuts, and cheese made from sheep or buffalo milk. Most villagers eat only poultry, fish, lamb, or beef once a week. Some Americanized versions of traditional Turkish dishes include pilaf (made of rice, almonds, meat, raisins and nuts), shish kebabs (pieces of lamb, tomatoes, peppers, and onions cooked together on a skewer), and the popular dessert, baklava (thin layers of pastry, honey, and chopped nuts). Eggplant is the primary vegetable. One stuffed eggplant dish, called *imam bayildi*, means "the priest fainted." The most common drinks are tea and strong, sweet coffee.

family picnic

Sports and Leisure

The Turks, if listing activities by priority, might place leisure and relaxation at the top. Village activities revolve around picnics, horse races, archery, and wrestling matches. The nation's favorite sport is soccer. Movies, concerts, plays, and operas are popular. Along the coast, people engage in yachting, water-skiing, snorkeling, and diving. Biking and mountain climbing are other possibilities. Ask any Turkish man his favorite form of relaxation, and he will point you to one of many coffeehouses where politics and business are discussed. However, if you are a woman, you will not be invited to join in!

Holidays and Celebrations

Many events and celebrations are based in Islam. *Kurban Bayrami* is a memorial to Abraham's experience of almost sacrificing Ishmael on Mt. Moriah.[47] This particular celebration is so important that the banks usually close for an entire week. *Seker Bayrami* is the feast celebrating the end of Ramadan, the holy month of fasting.

Secular holidays include the summer festivals of the International Istanbul Festival of Arts and Bursa's Music Festival. The Watermelon Festival in Diyarbakir is celebrated in September. On November 10 at 9:05 AM, the entire country stops for a moment to remember the death of Atatürk in 1938.

After learning about the great love and respect most Turks have for Atatürk, we are not surprised that the people's favorite holiday is *Egemenlik Bayrami* (National Sovereignty Day), celebrated on April 23. This holiday was declared by Atatürk in 1920 and is dedicated to children. Cities throughout the country enjoy the same type of activities on that day.

Perhaps the best way to understand the culture would be to visit and be part of this celebration. So, prepare to use your butterfly eyes and be part of the festivities!

Although the memory of Atatürk is honored, the children are the stars of the day. Entering the national soccer stadium we see children of all ages proudly wearing national costumes from the different areas of their country. Bright colors and sparkling trim magnify the joyful spirit of the day. Children have been rehearsing for weeks at their schools for this exciting time. It would be helpful to have butterfly wings, as well as eyes, in order to take in all the events in the stadium. Displays of dance, songs, poems, and plays are in abundance. Children from other parts of the world are invited to be part of the celebration.

This is a full day, and the stadium event is only one of many. We rush along with the crowd to the Atatürk Memorial and watch as people place flowers and sing the national anthem. Then, amid all the cheer and babble, complete quiet reigns for one full minute as respect is given to this favorite leader.

The day is not over, but in case we get hungry, we can take advantage of street stalls. The best choice is *kofte*,[48] a take-along sandwich that's easy to eat as we enjoy the celebration. Later we choose a snack of *simit*, made of dough and covered with sesame seeds, which looks a bit like our mall pretzels! And we cannot resist the Turkish candies made with pistachio nuts and honey.

The drinks are an interesting experience. Vendors wearing Ottoman costumes with big steel teapots on their backs sell sour cherry juice, or *visne suyu*. Or we might choose *sahlep*, a sweet milky

45

drink made of pulverized orchid root and sprinkled with cinnamon.

One other event we observe is the planting of trees. This activity by young scouts is a reminder to both children and adults of environmental issues. It also shows us that Turkey looks not only to the past but to the future as well.

April is the perfect time to enjoy Istanbul. Although we could choose another city, many say this is the place to start on any excursion into the culture of the Turks. The weather is pleasant this time of year; you seldom have to worry about rain. The celebration of Egemenlik Bayrami lasts only one day, but there are plenty of other sites to enjoy in this historic city. The ferries are a favorite mode of transportation or for a faster water ride, try the sea bus.

You may also see the Topkapi Palace, home to sultans from the 15th century until the 1800's. The harem grounds resemble a small village with plenty of room for the 300 or so concubines who once lived there.

Perhaps in this setting, we can truly understand the great sense of pride and national unity that is a part of Turkey 2000 and had its start centuries ago. These are a people who understand loyalty, joy, and hope in the future, and some are learning there is Someone who loves them even more than Atatürk did, someone who can bring even more profound changes to their lives. We think of the butterfly again, as a symbol of transformation.

The Other Turks

The Turks originally came from a land bordering the Mongolian Desert and the Caspian Sea, now called Turan. They arrived in Anatolia during the eleventh century.[49] Throughout history, they have scattered into other areas, always retaining their language. Today there are Turkish communities in Australia, Austria, Belgium, Egypt, France, Germany, the Netherlands, Saudi Arabia, Switzerland, Syria, Macedonia, Azerbaijan, Kazakstan, Kyrgyzstan, and Russia. The groups living outside of Turkey are predominantly Muslim, yet many have Christian resources available in their language.

Minority Groups in Turkey

The Kurds are the largest minority group in Turkey. Some estimate as many as 15 million Kurds in Turkey, the largest number in any one country in the Middle East. This ethnic group without a country still has great pride and a desire for a homeland. Their land of Kurdistan was divided among several countries at the end of World War I.

The south-central area of the country is home to as many as 1.5 million Arabs. Many live in the city of Adana. Accents and customs are different among this group.

Turkey Tidbits

Common sights:
- a fashionably dressed woman in a luxurious automobile
- a fully veiled woman in a horse drawn cart
- a sign in Arabic over the entrance to a mosque: "Good deeds cover bad deeds"
- the Whirling Dervish dancers of the Mevlana brotherhood[50]
- carpet-weaving in street side doorways and markets

Do's and Taboos
- women dress modestly in long skirts and long sleeves
- do remove shoes when visiting mosques
- do observe polite formalities when greeting or saying farewell to a host
- don't blow your nose in public
- don't show affection to the opposite gender in public
- don't point your finger at or show the bottom of your foot to anyone

Call to Prayer

Claim His promise: "Praise the Lord, all you nations, extol him, all you peoples. For great is his love toward us, and the faithfulness of the Lord endures forever" (Psalm 117:1,2 NIV).

Turkish family

PRAY for the children of Turkey. Ask God to give them inquisitive minds as they hear about Jesus Christ.

PRAY for the women of Turkey as they work and care for family members. Ask God to give them wisdom as they hear the Scriptures.

PRAY for the older generation to have a willingness to hear the new message without holding on to preconceived ideas of Christianity.

PRAY for God to make himself known to community leaders and government officials in miraculous ways.

PRAISE God for Turkish believers who are bold in sharing the gospel.

Chapter 4
Celebrating the Light

"Those who walked in the dark have seen a bright light. And it shines upon everyone who lives in the land of darkest shadows" (Isaiah 9:2 CEV).

A Parable

Content had lived in the darkness her entire life. Because of that, her eyes were accustomed to shadows and had adapted well. She had no problems doing her work or caring for her own needs and those of her family. She was now telling stories of the past to her children, just as her mother had told them to her. And life was good. There was no reason to wish for anything better.

Then one day it happened. A brightness streaked across her consciousness. It was so brief that she thought she was dreaming, for in her dreams there were colors and glitters. But surely she was only sleeping! It would be too overwhelming to be surrounded by light all the time! When she mentioned the event to her husband, *Resign*, he told her to be satisfied with her life. "Hasn't life always been good for our parents and all those before us? Why should we want something different?" he asked.

That made perfect sense to Content. So, when the momentary flashes came, she closed her eyes until they passed and was thankful for a simple world where things were decided and certain.

Then the children, *Hope* and *Promise*, ran to her one day with excitement in their young voices. "Mother," they chattered excitedly, "did you know there is a something very shiny and sparkly? It makes us feel so warm and happy! What is it, Mother?"

Quietly she took them on her lap and told them, "Sometimes things that seem quite real are only dreams, and sometimes things that appear better are really just different." And in the darkness she read to them from the dusty books of her parents and grandparents until they were calm.

Yet, somewhere deep inside her, deeper even than the center of her being, a spark was burning. Without really understanding, she knew she must step beyond the shadows and learn if there was a true light. She must discover if what she felt in the dreams could be trusted. And above all, she knew Hope and Promise would lead the way to the future.

The Truth Behind the Parable

"Turkey is a country full of history and rich Christian heritage," says Güney Gül, founder of Gül International, Inc., a ministry to Turks. "Today this country is smothered by the veil of Islam. It is a dark country where the light of the gospel of Jesus Christ has all but been extinguished . . . As few as 1,000 [Turks] are believers in Jesus Christ."

In fact, today the concept of a *Turkish Christian* is hard for the people to understand. For so long they have believed "To be a Turk is to be a Muslim." The secular government now allows freedom of religion. Why is the growth in accepting Christ so slow?

Stumbling blocks to Christianity are made not of stone, but of prejudice, bitterness, and misunderstanding.

1. The Crusades and other violent acts committed in the name of Christ have done almost irreparable damage.
2. It is socially acceptable to be a Muslim. Islam is recognized throughout the generations as the culturally appropriate religion.
3. The attitude toward anything Christian defeats many attempts at sharing Christ.
4. Press releases traditionally have spread negative and untrue stories about Christians. Some accuse Christians of consorting with terrorists groups and cults.
5. Religious persecution of Christian minorities in the past is remembered and still feared by some.
6. There are distortions and misunderstandings about Christian doctrine. Some of the most prevalent misconceptions are the Bible is filled of errors, Christians worship three gods (the Father, the Son, and the Holy Spirit or Mary), and the Christians believe God had sexual relations with Mary.
7. Television is another stumbling block. Turks see a negative representation of Western culture and believe it is based on Christian values. They have no desire to pollute their society with these "Christian" ways.

Cities in Turkey are still surrounded by ruins of ancient walls. One believer from the United States says he feels the ruins of walls around Istanbul and other cities in Turkey are symbolic of the walls that keep the people from hearing the gospel. He lists three *walls*:

1. *the wall of ritual*, built of the meaningless acts that are part of the religion, but not faith;
2. *the wall of resources or material wealth* which entraps those who have lost faith in the Muslim concept of God but know nothing of the Christian God; and

3. *the wall of repression* which often comes from friends and family who discourage those seeking to learn about Christianity.

This believer suggests that the gospel will enter Turks' lives through the "gate" of personal relationships. "It is only through establishing solid relationships with the Turks that we can hope to lead them from the darkness that envelopes them and to tear down the strongholds of the enemy that persist in that land," he explains.

The Good News

With all of this in mind, are you ready for the good news? Well, get ready to celebrate!

Nearly 2,000 years ago Paul led the way to take the gospel to present-day Turkey. Met with resistance and persecution, God's work persisted, grew and flourished. Churches were established in key cities, including the seven churches mentioned in Revelation.[51]

Historical events brought Islam to the country and the bright fire of the early church almost died out. But in the 1960s, the light again took hold in Turkey, and today the future of the church and its outreach to unbelievers is growing bright.

Many Turks are in a time of cultural transition. They are open to new ideas about life in general, including religion. The power of God's word is at work in this atmosphere. Translations of the New Testament are available in modern Turkish, and a translation of the Old Testament in modern Turkish is currently in the works. Estimates are that a half a million or more copies have been distributed along with Bible correspondence courses and the *Jesus* film. Celebrate!

There were only ten known Turk believers in 1960. In 1993 there were at least twelve Turkish-speaking fellowships and exciting news of more than 4,000 new Turkish-speaking Christians in Bulgaria.[52] However, today exact estimates of both congregations and believers in Turkey are difficult to ascertain. Part of the reason is a good one: they are increasingly responsive to God's word and growing too fast to count! Celebrate!

The need to train new believers is being met slowly. Tyrannus School, the first full-time ministry training center in evangelism and discipleship, was started by a Turkish Christian couple. They are inspired with a vision to equip the Turks to reach their nation.[53] Celebrate!

Güney Gül, a former Muslim from Turkey, produces 15-20 minute gospel messages that are broadcast by radio in Turkey and surrounding countries. Potentially, millions of people may hear this Turkish gospel presentation daily. These are well-received because they are contemporary in music and tone. Celebrate!

In 1993, it was estimated that more than five million pieces of Christian literature have been distributed through personal contact, postal evangelism, and advertisements in the Turkish press.[54] Celebrate!

> Paul was called a troublemaker when he preached at Thessalonica. He was accused of "turning the world upside down" (Acts 17:6 KJV).
> The homes of many Turks were turned upside down quite literally on August 17, 1999. It was a dark day. Who could imagine what light was about to break through!

The Earthquake Opens Doors and Opens Hearts

Only God could bring good out of the devastation that visited the western part of Turkey on August 17, 1999. Some areas of Istanbul sustained damage, but Izmit, Golcuk, Adapazari suffered the most destruction and greatest loss of life.

Only those who lived through the devastation and the days that followed can give us accounts that are true and accurate. The following paragraphs are true stories of earthquake victims and survivors shared by Christian relief workers. Open your heart to their stories. Find the cause for celebration!

Figen's Story[55]

A counselor at a tent camp in Turkey, shared the following story:

"On August 31, 1999, a 15-year-old girl named Figen came to the counseling tent to talk to someone about some recurring dreams. Figen said that she had been having the same dream every night for the last year and just wanted to tell someone about it. In her dream, she saw a man in shining clothes riding a white horse. He had eyes of fire and what looked like a sword of fire in his right hand. He and the horse were on a large staircase with many steps. Figen said that the man was everything that was good, pure, just, holy, and perfect. Each night as she would dream this dream, the man on the horse would descend one step and would say to her, 'I am coming down to lift you up, fear not, I will rescue you.' Figen was aware that she was on the other side of a very deep chasm that separated her from the man on the horse; she said that there were shadowy figures with bloodstained hands holding her and many others from approaching the man in shining clothes.

"Figen then went on to tell about the other dream that the man in shining clothes had given her. Each night for one week before the earthquake, she was shown in a dream the devastation that was about to come on her town. She tried to warn her family and others that there was going to be a terrible earthquake in a few days, but no one would listen to her. Her mother even slapped her and told her she was demon possessed. Again, the night of the earthquake, she tried to warn but no one would listen. Of course the earthquake happened as it was shown to her by the man on the horse.

"Figen said that the man on the horse had truly rescued her—he had saved her life. She said that she would do anything for him because he was everything that is good. He said that he now lived in her heart forever. He also showed her what her future would be. She would work for him by reaching out to children all over the world and telling about what he had done for her. He also showed her that she would suffer many things because she followed him. Figen said that she did not care if she suffered for him because he is so wonderful and good."

Christians who worked at the counseling tent then told Figen that the man on the horse was Jesus, the risen Savior and One whom they serve.

Read Revelation 19:11 and following.[56] Many have found the Lord through dreams. God is powerful and cannot be put in a box to meet our small ideas and expectations. We can celebrate His work in Figen's life!

The following stories are of earthquake victims who were treated and ministered to through a prosthetics program sponsored by Turkish World Outreach.

S.D.[57]

S.D., a middle-aged Turkish woman, was trapped under her wardrobe for 43 hours. Her foot was doubled up under her leg, and when she was finally rescued, doctors first amputated above the knee, and then had to remove the entire leg.

S.D. lost her husband and two sons in the earthquake, and everything she owned in her house. She also lost many friends. Nonetheless, S.D. holds her emotions inside and tries to keep herself from crying. She now lives with her older brother.

A.[58]

This woman was visiting her best friend the night of the earthquake. Their building collapsed, and her friend survived only a few hours. A. was trapped under the body of her friend for 24 hours until a soldier found her and brought her water and a machine lifted the crushed wall off of her. A.'s leg was amputated above the knee, and she spent 20 days on a dialysis machine to save her kidneys.

C.A.[59]
This 28-year-old woman was caught under concrete for nine hours while her foot was bent backwards and crushed. During this time, she worried about her seven-year-old daughter who, as she later discovered, died in the tragic event.

C.A.'s husband survived with minor wounds. C.A. and her husband believe this event was God's will and that they shouldn't complain. When they received medical treatment from Christian workers, a Christian shared with them about God's compassion and grief for their loss and His love for them and their daughter.

> "The devastating earthquake . . . has shaken more than the buildings. There is unprecedented opportunity for the Kingdom of God in Turkey."
> –Jayson Knox, the International Turkey Network

New Believers and Young Churches Meet Crisis with Boldness
"The small but growing national church stepped forward in bold, wise leadership of earthquake relief efforts," relates Jayson Knox of the International Turkey Network.

The national press and television gave positive coverage of Christian work related to the earthquake.

Jayson added: "The earthquake's effect was felt in many areas. Turkish converts often face hardships and harassment aimed at silencing their witness. But when the earthquake hit, the Jesus that lived in them knew what to do. The Holy Spirit gave them opportunities to witness and they were confident and bold. It was like watching the rebirth of the book of Acts. God has used this trouble to transform the church."

Doors Continue to Open
In December 1999, police raided one Turkish church, arresting 40 members and locking the doors. Later, authorities encouraged the church to reopen. They were allowed to hold a citywide Christmas celebration. More than 1,300 people saw a play about the birth, life, death, and resurrection of Christ. During the same month, President Demirel made Turkish history as the first head of state to send Christmas greetings to Christians.

"Government officials are more tolerant of Christianity lately because churches and international ministries have been central in providing relief after last year's earthquakes," said a report from Compass Direct in January 2000.

The love and joy Turks found in the Christian community as they fellowshiped and worshiped influenced some who became believers. During the quake, they asked, "Why is it always the Christians who come to help? Why not our Muslim brothers?"

Need more reasons to celebrate? Read what Christians who are related to the work in Turkey have to say.

Nanci Celebrates[60]

"[God] taught me to humble myself before Him and trust Him in all things. My journey to Istanbul has challenged me to be bolder in my walk with God. I pray my life will reflect the joy He has put in my heart. I now have a burden for the unreached nations."

David Celebrates[61]

"This outreach exemplified how [God's work] needs to be done. God gives us a vision, and we work together to see it through to completion . . . [We] can partner together with our own churches and others to see Christ's Kingdom established among all the nations of the earth."

These Turkish Christians share why they are celebrating.
Timothy[62] *Celebrates*
Timothy is a Turkish man who was brought up in Turkey in a close, Muslim family. He first stared learning about Islam at an early age: "You learn it from your family, friends, relatives, the society, school, etc." Timothy was taught there was one true God, Allah, and one uncorrupted scripture, the Al Qur'an.

Later Timothy read the passages in the Al Qur'an which mentioned the biblical scriptures and was curious about them. He eventually learned about Jesus through a Bible correspondence course. Timothy wrote to some people and they sent him books explaining Christianity and certain related topics. "When I read those books the first time, I didn't take them very seriously," he said. "But when I thought of what I had read, I had to have deeper thoughts and ask God for guidance."

Timothy explained that he was confused by the concepts of the Trinity, Jesus being the Son of God and God Himself, the idea of revelation, and the connection between Christianity and Judaism. He also had to hide these materials from his family and friends. "When I revealed them to them, they were scared that these materials would change my mind, and they wanted to protect me," recalls Timothy.

"Some friends borrowed some of the books and later on they did not return them because they told me they burned them."

Eventually, the Holy Spirit convinced Timothy of who Jesus is and how salvation could reconcile him with God. As a new Christian, Timothy still had struggles: "I was in my hometown in Turkey. It was difficult because I didn't know any other Christians and didn't know what to do next." He also added, "It was a very strange feeling being in a church [the first time], not knowing what to do and how to act and talk to the other Christians . . . [but] they were very warm and welcoming."

Timothy asks for prayer for his parents and for his future service for the Lord. He also gives advice on how to minister to Turks and Muslims: "The most important point is to be a true friend and show Jesus' love—basically practicing what we preach."

Güney Celebrates
Güney Gül was born in Istanbul. His parents divorced when he was young, and his mother was ill. When he was 15, his mother moved to Holland and remarried another Turkish man. "My stepfather and I did not get along at all," says Güney. "My real father sent me an airplane ticket to Florida when I was about 18 years old. I came to the USA and lived with my father for three years." In America, Güney attended church for one and a half years yet says no one ever witnessed to him. Later on he became friends with a Jewish girl who was saved through a Bible study and invited Güney to attend also.

Güney learned that Jesus was more than a prophet and was touched by John 3:16. "I found out that I could for sure go to heaven. In Islam you do not have this assurance. Christianity offers heaven because Jesus lives in heaven." Güney realized he had to make a decision and after two months of asking questions and talking with pastors, he believed Jesus was his Savior and no longer followed Mohammed.

"When I told my real father that I had become a Christian, he yelled at me all night long and said I should be killed," said Güney. When he told his mother, she cried but still loved and accepted him. "Last year Mom told me that she had had a dream before she was pregnant with me that she was in her house. A group of people came, carried her down the hill, laughing and rejoicing . . . She saw a glass coffin, and in it she saw Jesus—He was smiling, not in pain but in peace," related Güney. "She talked to her father, a Muslim, about the dream and he said, 'You saw the prophet Jesus, and He must have favor in you. You will have a son, and Jesus will have favor in your son. This son is going to be very important for Jesus—He will shine out through him."

Today, Güney heads Gül International, Inc., a ministry which reaches out to Turks around the world with gospel radio programs. "The Lord gave me a vision to reach out to the Turk people by radio," he says.

A celebration is in order when something out of the ordinary takes place. Current interest in the message of Jesus Christ in the nation of Turkey is truly extraordinary. However, it is not surprising.

According to Jayson Knox at the International Turkey Network, there were more than 4,000 prayer walkers in Turkey during Prayer through the Window in October 1999 alone. He refers to Revelation 8:4, 5 in the wake of the earthquake: "the prayers of the saints went up before God from the angel's hand. Then the angel took the censer, filled it with fire from the altar and hurled it on the earth; and there came peals of thunder, rumblings, flashes of lightening and an earthquake."

Turkey has experienced not only a natural disaster; but also a spiritual earthquake.

Things to Consider as You Celebrate

Dwight, a Christian from Georgia, spent several weeks in Turkey with the Muslim people. Let his experience enrich your perspective:

"The reality is that the majority of Muslims are no different from our neighbors or us, with the exception of some obvious cultural differences . . . We both simply want to make the best life for ourselves and the ones we love . . . We both sincerely desire to know the God who created us, perhaps they more so than most Americans.

"The difference is that I am blessed enough to live in a part of the world where the gospel is freely preached, and it is safe to adhere to its message. Most Muslims in Turkey and the rest of the Middle East have never heard about the grace of Jesus, and those who have are fearful to respond. Let us not be quick to judge those who have never been given any alternative."[63]

It is easy to settle into our own personal comfort zone. It is natural to resist change when we don't know the outcome or when danger is a perceived possibility. However, it is also true that God has placed in every human heart the ability to hope and to respond to a promise presented with love and power.

Turkey Tidbits

- The goal of Christians in Turkey is to have a church in each of Turkey's 102 provinces.
- It is possible to give away thousands of Turkish New Testaments to interested Turks in the marketplaces of the cities.
- In the 1999 earthquake . . .
  . . . more than 17,000 people died.
  . . . at least 50,000 were injured.
  . . . more than 200,000 were left homeless.[64]

- Hope International Church in Istanbul bought a water truck to help take clean drinking water to cities after the quake.[65]
- Christian workers distributed $50,000 worth of food, soap, diapers, and other items in the quake areas.[66]

Call to Prayer

Claim His promise: ". . . if you call out for insight and cry aloud for understanding, and if you look for it as for silver and search for it as for hidden treasure, then you will understand the fear of the Lord and find the knowledge of God: (Proverbs 3:5 NIV).

PRAY for the recovering victims of the 1999 earthquakes to continue a contact with those who offered both physical and spiritual hope to them.

PRAY for Turkish Christians to have insight into God's plans for them and be willing to follow His directions.

PRAY for mature Christians to answer the call to disciple and mentor new believers.

PRAY for the leaders in mobilization to have wisdom in knowing how to find and use resources for the work.

PRAY for safety and health for those on short-term service in Turkey at this time.

PRAISE God for the giftedness He places in each of His people and for His guidance to every one of us.

Southern Baptist and other Christian volunteers are among the first to arrive to offer relief after the 1999 earthquakes in Turkey.

Chapter 5
Illuminating the Future

"Your mighty power is a light for all nations" (Luke 2:32a CEV).

God's Available Power

We can look into the future and offer hope and a promise, not because of anything we are or anything we do, but because of the mighty power of God.

The Power of God in Creation
"The earth is the Lord's and everything in it, the world and all who live in it; for he founded it upon the seas and established it upon the waters" (Psalm 24:1,2 NIV).

God formed the Anatolian peninsula at the beginning of time. It was not more or less important than other parts of the world, but it was placed strategically as a link between the continent of Europe and the Near East. He made no mistake when he formed the high plateau surrounded by steep mountain ranges (Psalm 65:6). He prepared the areas where crops would grow and sheep would pasture (Psalm 65:13). He designed it so that coastal cities would become busy harbors for ships and trade (Psalm 104:9). Turkey was in His vision when He said, "That's good!" The sun He placed in the sky was as surely for the benefit and pleasure of this land as for that of any state in your country, any country in the world.

The Power of God in History
"He rules forever by his power, his eyes watch the nations—let not the rebellious rise up against him" (Psalm 66:7 NIV).

Thinking back to the history of Turkey (Chapter 1) we may be puzzled at the events and the many different nations and peoples as they played across the scenes of time. The Hittites, Greeks, Persians, Romans . . . what was their part in the unfolding drama? Why was the Christian message in bondage for years? Perhaps we find some answers in Revelation. Others we have to wait for. All we know, and really all we need to know, is that God is in control and has always been in control (Psalm 135:6, Isaiah 14:27). How finite our vista and infinitesimal our grasp of time and space! Read Isaiah 40 to adjust the perspective.

The Power of God in His People
"For we do not preach ourselves, but Jesus Christ as Lord, and ourselves as your servants for Jesus' sake. For God, who said, "Let light
shine out of darkness," made his light shine in our hearts to give us
the light of the knowledge of the glory of God in the face of Christ"
(2 Corinthians 4:5-6 NIV).

*It is interesting that Paul probably wrote these words to the church at
Corinth while he was in Ephesus. How many times have we been comfort-
ed by the following sentences that assure us that even with our rough,
plain clay pots, God's surpassing power is available (2 Corinthians 4:7)!
What an amazing thing that God has chosen us to be co-workers with
Him (1 Corinthians 3:9) and promised He will make us ready and able to
do what He calls us to do (Philippians 2:13)! God's people have been
faithful through different times, locations, and ways to minister and witness in dark places. God has been faithful to use His people for His glory.
Hence, we have a message of light to share (1 John 1:5).*

The Power of God in the Future
"Now to him who is able to do immeasurably more than all we ask
or imagine, according to his power that is at work within us, to him
be glory in the church and in Christ Jesus throughout all generations,
for ever and ever! Amen" (Ephesians 3:20 NIV).

Did you get it? Forever and ever? Amen, indeed!

God's power is proven through creation (Isaiah 48:13), through
history (Psalm 118:16), and through His people (Acts 1:8). Because
of what we know of the past and because of what we experience in
the present, we can claim a future filled with His works and electri-
fied with His power (Isaiah 43:13).

God's Available People
Webster's Dictionary gives several definitions of *available* that are
interesting to apply them to God's people.
• ready for immediate use
• qualified or willing to do something
• willing to assume a responsibility

Through the power of the Holy Spirit, we can have the attitudes
and attributes that will keep us fresh and usable in His work. We can
be full of joy, peace, patience, kindness, goodness, faithfulness, gen-
tleness, and self-control (Galatians 5:23).

To be ready for immediate use, we cannot carry around the bag-
gage of unrepented sin or a heart cold from indifference. We must
stay *prayed up with passport in hand*! We must be willing to search
God's Word and the daily news for direction as we stay available.

When God gives us opportunity to learn a new skill or expand our knowledge, it could be in preparation for a future assignment. We dare not be lazy or complacent. The ability He gives us to grow has an accountability factor.

To say we are willing is only truthful when we set no limits. The words *except*, *unless*, and *no* are incompatible with a willing spirit. To be completely and unequivocally willing is one of life's best faith-stretchers!

People who are willing to assume a responsibility are greatly needed in today's world. It isn't always considered smart to take responsibility for even your own actions and welfare if you can get by more easily without it. To see a need that is beyond you and respond to that need is past understanding; but the peace God promised will accompany such faith is also unexplainable (Philippians 4:7).

Being Available through Prayer

Why pray? Because God listens, we must pray all the days we live (Psalm 116:2). How long shall we pray? There is no time to stop in our petitions (I Thessalonians 5:17).

In the streets of Turkey, the call to prayer echoes five times each day to alert devout followers of Islam. The minaret attached to the outside of the mosque is a conical tower used by the crier, or *muezzin*, to send out this call to prayer. God is calling Christians from across the world to pray for the nation of Turkey and its people.

In the early 1990s, the 10/40 window concept enabled Christians to begin a concentrated prayer focus on Turkey. According to Jayson Knox of the International Turkey Network, during October 1999 alone, more than 4000 prayer walkers have gone to claim the power of God's love through cities and villages, along modern streets and country pathways.

Dwight, a prayer walker from a church in Georgia, states, "We may send thousands to speak the gospel . . . distribute a million Bibles . . . build relationships with every person in the city, but without the power of God that is unleashed by the prayers of His people, the walls of the enemy will persist. Prayer is the single greatest weapon that we possess, yet it may be the least utilized. Never feel that praying is 'the least that I can do,' for it is truly the most you can do!"[67]

Developing a Prayer Strategy

The question is not if you should pray for Turkey, but how you will develop a vital prayer link with that area. Resources for the following strategies are listed at the end of this chapter.

Planning for Personal Prayer Involvement

Which of these ideas can you build on in your personal prayer time? These are starting points. God will impress on you how to pray as you mold your thoughts to His.

Commitment

Make a deliberate choice to pray specifically for the country of Turkey and the Turkish people there and around the world. Make a pledge to yourself to do this. Read the quotation just preceding this section on prayer if you need a reminder of the importance of this promise.

Consistency

Let prayer become a good habit. Keep at it. Be persistent and firm in your focus. How important is this, in your opinion? Does it go beyond a Monday-Wednesday-Friday tag-on to your established prayer time? Will it be a continuing conversation piece with God?

Compassion

Move beyond just being sorry about circumstances that happen to someone else. Add a desire to make a difference in situations. See past numbers to faces. Look with God's eyes.

Content

Pray with substance. Couple the feeling of compassion with the knowledge of facts. Be specific. Find resources in order to stay current in your prayer quest. Make a *Turkey* folder with news clippings, notes from articles, and other information that comes to you.

Creativity

Use your unique skills, thought processes, and lifestyle to nudge yourself into prayer. Think quickly about five impressions you may have at this very moment about Turkey. Jot them down before they fly away. They don't have to be deeply spiritual or religious. For instance, maybe you think of the nation's passion with soccer. Great! Every time you see a soccer score in the news, an advertisement for the sport, or a child's ball, let it trigger an instant prayer response. Choose a reminder which works for you. Maybe it will be when you add olives at the salad bar or see a street vendor.

Planning for Corporate Prayer

God may ask you to lead or encourage others to join in on this prayer adventure. Where two or more come together for a specific purpose of prayer, His work is honored, and your voice is multiplied.

Who might be interested?
Start with those with whom you already have prayer connections: your prayer partner or partners, your family, people in groups at church, or your circle of friends. Don't forget others who have been exposed to the information in this study. Remember that children and youth have also been focusing on this area of the world and on prayer in their study materials.

Where do we start?
Start with those involved. Discuss as a family if you can add this to a prayer time you have already established. Add it to the list you share with your prayer partners and explain why this is on your heart. Talk with your pastor or other church leaders. Discuss a year-long plan[68] to pray for Turkey which may be launched with this emphasis. Offer to share specific requests and information.

What is missing?
Sometimes we get bogged down in the obvious and don't see the whole picture. What about a study/prayer group during lunch breaks once a week at work? If you have a ministry at a retirement village or assisted living complex this could be a link with some great and seasoned pray-ers.

How can I do all this?
You can't do it yourself. That's not the plan. God's strength is yours and God's people are co-workers with you and with Him. But God may want your voice to activate the ideas.

Finally, pray for Turkey as if it is a matter of life and death. It is!

To keep up with current prayer needs and updates on the ministry in Turkey, consider receiving *Light in the Darkness,* an email newsletter written by Christians in Turkey. To receive the newsletter, contact turkeypartner@iname.com.

You may also want to contact the International Mission Board, the International Turkey Network, Turkish World Outreach, or your associational or state Baptist headquarters and WMU for materials on prayer for Turkey, prayer consultations, and prayer-related trips. Contact information is listed at the end of this chapter.

Being Available through Other Opportunities for Active Participation

Just to be clear, prayer is an *active* participation in the work God is doing in Turkey; but it is not the *only* type of participation available. The following are experiences for which you can pray. See the resource list at the end of this chapter for ways to make contact and get more information about any of the listed programs.

The Ministry/Witness of Writing

Some argue that letter writing is a lost art. Telephones and electronic communications have erased the need for *snail mail*. Not so! To take a blank piece of paper and share things about what you think and what is important to you is a tool to break barriers and build understanding. Consider these possibilities.

Pen Friend Ministry, Gül International, Inc.

People in Turkey are eager to learn English and to learn about America. An advertisement offering Pen Friends to correspond was placed in a Turkish newspaper. A year-and-a-half later, requests are still coming from both children and adults. Sometimes five requests come in one day. There is often a waiting list. Güney Gül, founder of the program, states, "One by one as Christian youth and adults reach out in friendship to these people, they will have the opportunity to share the gospel with their friend."

The Pen Friend Ministry is important because it reaches many children. It will have an impact on the future of our world as they begin to understand one another and care about people from other places. They are a starting point to unite the nations of the world.

When children write, Güney rejoices that they are so eager and open to learning: "Children do not know any language or nationalities barrier."

What an opportunity! Touch a child, touch a world.

Turkish Pen-Friends, Turkish World Outreach

Adults and students ages eleven and above can have pen-friends and share the gospel with them. Addresses come through English teachers in Turkey, and all the correspondence is in English. Most who request these letters are between the ages of 13–19, but there are also some adults. This ministry tries to match pen friends by age group and interests.

Each Christian receives guidelines to help in sharing Christ. A few minutes a month and a small amount in postage cost can be a great investment for the Kingdom work.

This is also a great way to learn about Turkish customs and culture and encourage spiritual growth. It can lead to further prayer and involvement.

"We have to limit the number of letters we send to English teachers in Turkey, because we would have too many requests and not enough Christians to assign to them," comments Steve Hagerman of Turkish World Outreach (TWO).

Gospel Letters to Turks, Turkish World Outreach
"Can you help?" asks Steve Hagerman. "We urgently need Christian volunteers who will send ten Gospel Letters per month to Muslim families in Turkey."

Turkish World Outreach (TWO) has three million addresses and is praying for a Gospel Letter Volunteer for each one. Turkish letters, a translation, addresses, and instructions are provided. Volunteers provide postage[69] and envelopes.

These letters offer a free Turkish New Testament and Jesus Film video as well as a free Bible correspondence course to those interested. The program is evangelical and non-sectarian. TWO works with Campus Crusade for Christ and Operation Mobilization, as well as other ministry organizations in Turkey.

> "Several hundred Turks respond to our Gospel Letters each year
> . . . In a survey a few years ago, 85 percent of Turkish converts
> said their first contact with the gospel was through one of these
> letters," adds Steve Hagerman.

Are you wondering how much impact a ministry of writing can have? Perhaps this information will answer your question and concern.

Here are excepts from some letters from people in Turkey sent in response to the Gospel Letters:[70]

"The letter you mailed to me surprised me . . . We are pleased to learn about and become acquainted with the Injil (New Testament) and Jesus Christ . . . I am certain that through your help the truth of this topic will come to us."—Mr. and Mrs. H.K.

"When I received your letter, I was very surprised and without hope. I was pleased when your letter arrived at the time I felt in the greatest need . . . I live in the midst of strong Muslim believers . . . I would like you to pray about these things."—Ms. L.B.

"The Kurdish people are oppressed . . . Your letter was a sunlight, a light, a hope in our darkness . . . We request a holy Injil (New Testament) and a free video which explains the life of Christ."—Mr. and Mrs. N. and I.G

"I admire your religion . . . Christianity pushes me to think . . . I am the father of six children. I especially want more information about Jesus Christ . . . All of us love you very much. Pray for us."—Mr. M. U.

"I got your most valued letter, and I was very pleased. I am making a minimum of 1000 copies of this letter and preparing to distribute them . . . I am working to make it safe for believers . . . "—Mr. H.A.

"I prevented my friend from destroying your letter, took it from his hands, and read it. I am the daughter of a Muslim family. We believed that other religions were evil lies. Your letter opened my eyes . . . I want to leave [Islam] and follow the path of Jesus Christ. I will follow the commands of Jesus Christ until death."—Miss I.D.

The Ministry/Witness of Strategic Partnerships
Short-Term Project
The short-term project is a tool to help churches see the big picture of God's desire for Christians to go and tell others about Christ. Sending, praying, and giving are each important and necessary in taking the gospel to Turkey and to the entire world; but there is no substitute for doing the work, as well.

Chip, a minister from Georgia, says mobilizers are needed to develop environments within the church that will nurture hearts and prepare people to fulfill the Great Commission.

If your church is interested in developing a partnership to focus on the people of Turkey, send an email to turkeypartner@iname.com and ask for an information packet.

The short-term volunteer can fill many specialized areas in Turkey. One of the most important is that of prayer walking. It is apparent that God has used this ministry to make the hearts of the people ready to hear the gospel. Short-term volunteers can also use their skills or interest to supplement the time and energy of those involved in working full-time in Turkey.

It is possible for short-term teams to spend concentrated effort in prayer and Bible distribution, leaving the follow-up work to Christians living in the area. Short-term workers can provide the footwork needed to establish new fellowship groups. The key is to support the ongoing ministry/witness by the Turk Christians.

Long-Term Relationships
It is vital to couple short-term projects with ongoing relationships of support and prayer. Acts 13 is the model for this strategy. A strong base is needed to provide financial help in this ministry. Seldom does a church or an individual who is involved in short-term ministry withdraw from that ministry. They just adapt their strategy. Actually, the limited journey provides the fuel to keep the fire going on that field and also fans the flames in the local church area.

Life Transplants
Sometimes God not only says, "Go," but He also says, "Stay there." There are places waiting for those people whom God has called to plant their lives in Turkey. Some possibilities include ministering to people through serving them and sharing God's truth with them. The Turkish people are remarkably open to discussing their faith. There are a wide variety of ministry opportunities in Turkey.

Any skill, interest, or ability you have can be tempered and molded to God's use. He has gifted you and prepared you for the place He calls you to serve.

Additional Opportunities
Perhaps there are reasons none of these seem like your special place in God's Great Commission plan. God's methods, just as His resources, are truly limitless.

Both tape and radio ministries can use people with specific areas of expertise. Most organizations can use volunteers who are willing to do office work—from answering phones to doing mail outs to trouble-shooting computer problems. If God places a passion in your heart for the Turks and you cannot go there, watch diligently. He may send them to you. Be involved in ministries through your college campus, church, or community to teach English. Be alert to pockets of people from various countries.

Are you curious about the effect of serving on a short-term team in Turkey? Consider these first-hand reports from members of a church in Georgia who joined a short-term prayer walking team.[71]

Caroline
"I learned that prayer is not important; it is absolutely essential . . .
For at least 17 years, I have been involved in [fulfilling the Great
Commission] through prayer, financial support, and educating others
. . . This trip allowed me to see in a different, very relevant way the
desperateness of the lost . . . I used to wonder how God could use
people who went on trips for such a short time . . . [Our] excited atti-
tude can be used of God to fan the flame of long-term [personnel].

David
"My life was changed forever as I learned to listen to God's voice . . .
As I walked through the city of 15 million, I could almost hear Jesus
say, 'I died for every face you see . .. .' God showed me that people
all over the world need Jesus, and He needs obedient children to
carry the message.

Cindy
"Now I have seen with my eyes the *other* people whom God loves.
My capacity to care was limited by lack of exposure to the fact that
God is the Creator of *all* peoples. He has awakened a passion and
concern for those who are so different from me."

Tim
"I learned how important prayer walking is while in Turkey. I have
started doing this for my neighborhood (something I would never
have done prior). God has made me more aware of people and more
sensitive to their needs. I have committed to reach out to lost souls I
meet to help them find the greatest gift they could ever receive."

God's Available Call
You have experienced God's call before. He spoke to you individually
and specifically when you came to recognize Jesus as your Lord and
Savior. Isn't it strange that each of us hears God in a different way?
There are no cookie-cutter salvation experiences in Christianity!

Or maybe it's not so strange. If you are a parent, you know how it
is to give the same message in various ways to your different children. One child may be sensitive and seems ready to listen and hears
you quickly, responding readily. For another there is reluctance and
for still another a questioning spirit. You speak to them differently—
not because you love one more but because you love each the most.
You tailor the way you communicate to the way you know each one
will comprehend.

God knows us better than we know our own children! God's communication to us continues, and He calls us to new adventures with Him. That has always been His plan for His people.

God called Abraham to leave home and go far away, and Abraham went, unsure of what it would mean yet willingly.[72] God called a reluctant Moses and gave him Aaron to help with his missions.[73] He called Joshua to be a bold leader and promised him success if he would be obedient.[74] God called Samuel and kept calling him until he listened.[75] He called Paul to be a missionary—to go and preach the Word.[76]

God sends a call to Christians today to reach out to a world in darkness. With the call comes a command and a promise: "Be strong and courageous. Do not be terrified; do not be discouraged, for the Lord your God will be with you wherever you go" (Joshua 1:9 NIV).

Even to Turkey, Lord?

". . . to the ends of the earth" (Acts 1:8 NIV).

Organizations to Help You Become Involved in Reaching Turkey

International Mission Board
P.O. Box 6767
Richmond, VA 23230
• general information: www.ibm.org
• volunteer opportunities: 1-800-888-8657
• PrayerLink/PrayerPlus: 1-888-462-7729 or prayer.plus@imb.org
• PeopleLink: 1-877-462-4721

International Turkey Network
655 E. University Drive
Mesa, AZ 85203

Turkish World Outreach
Box 3098
Grand Junction, CO 81504

Gül International, Inc.
1704 Frederica Road, #627
St. Simons Island, GA 31522
(912) 634-6048
guney@btconline.net

Prayer Newsletter for Turkey
turkeypartner@iname.com

Check www.womenonmission.com for a section called "Loving Muslim Women through Prayer."

State and Association Baptist or WMU Offices
(Contact your pastor or WMU Director for information.)

Turkey Tidbits

- The mayor of one Turkish city has requested that someone come and start an international church.
- The Turkish gospel radio program is available to the 200,000 Turkish people living in Lebanon and Australia as well as those in Turkey.
- Most Turkish Christians come from a modern rather than traditional segment of society.
- As many as half of the Turks who become believers turn away within two years; the need for discipleship is critical.
- For as little as 60 cents, you can mail a Gospel Letter to someone in Turkey and possibly open contact between that person and a Turkish Christian there.

Call to Prayer

Claim His promise: "Devote yourselves to prayer, being watchful and thankful. And pray for us, too, that God may open a door for our message, so that we may proclaim the mystery of Christ . . .." (Colossians 4:2, 3 NIV).

PRAY for the leadership of each of the organizations listed under the resource section above.

PRAY for those involved in the writing opportunities—both for those who send and who receive letters.

PRAY for a great army of prayers to be impressed with the urgency of holding up this great venture with God daily.

PRAY that the people God is calling to go with short-term teams to Turkey will be available to answer that call.

PRAY for understanding and willingness as you search to find God's personal call to you and His corporate call to your church in this partnership of faith sharing.

PRAY for new Turkish believers to grow in God's Word and be the spiritual leaders of their people.

PRAISE God for all He has done across the years to prepare both the proclaimers and the receivers of His Word.

Endnotes

[1] Cranfill, Caroline. *Doors of Opportunity: A Publication of First Baptist Church Woodstock, Georgia* (1999).

[2] www.twarp.com/titr/Hi.htm

[3] Ibid.

[4] www. exploreturkey.com/anadolu.htm

[5] Biblical references to the Hittites include: Genesis 10:15; 1 Chronicles 1:13; Gen. 23; Gen. 25:7-11; Gen. 49:32; Exodus 23:23,28; 32:2; 34:11; Deut. 7:1; Joshua 3:10; Numbers 13:29; Deut. 20:17; Josh. 9:1; 11:3; 12:8; 24:11; Judges 1:26; 3:5; 1 Kings 9:20; 2 Chronicles 8:7; 1 Kings 10:29; 2 Chronicles 1:17; 1 Kings 11:1-2; Ezra 9:1-3.

[6] *The World Book Encyclopedia*, Vol. 19. Chicago: World Book, Inc., 1996, p. 509.

[7] www.twarp.com/titr/tt1.htm

[8] Exodus 1-15

[9] www.turkishodyssey.com/turkey/history/history2.htm

[10] Acts 13-14

[11] Acts 15:36-18:18

[12] Acts 18:23-20:6

[13] The modern city of Selçuk or Efes.

[14] Rev. 2-3

[15] See note 9 above.

[16] a Muslim people from Central Asia

[17] from 1243 to the early 1300s

[18] "The term Ottoman is a dynastic appellation derived from the Arabic Uthman (Turkish: Osman), the name of the warrior ruler who is regarded as the founder of both dynasty and empire." (Goetz, Philip W., ed. *The New Encyclopedia Britannica*, Macropaedia, Vol. 28, 15th Edition. Chicago: Enclyclopedia Britannica, Inc., 1985, p. 915.)

[19] "In their initial stages of expansion, the Ottomans were leaders of the Turkish gazis, or fighters for the faith of Islam, against the shrinking Christian Byzantine state." (Ibid.)

[20] www.calpoly.edu/~pkiziria/pub-files/history.html

[21] "The Tanzimat is the name given to the series of Ottoman reforms promulgated during the reigns of Mahmud's sons." (Ibid., 930.)

[22] "The young officers who had made the revolution, like their civilian supporters, were primarily concerned with preserving the Ottoman Empire; they feared that Hamidian policies and European interventions were endangering its existance." (Ibid.,, p. 932.)

[23] Ibid.

[24] "Possibly a million Armenians either fled or were killed (principally by Kurdish irregulars) or deported." (Ibid., p. 933.)

[25] "In his declaration of July 12, 1947, Inonu stated that the logic of a multiparty system implied the possibility of a change of government. Prophetically, he renounced the title of 'National Unchangeable Leader,' which had been conferred upon him in 1938." (Ibid., p. 935.)

[26] Ibid., p. 936

[27] The Kurds represent about 14-19% of the population of Turkey. They are "an Indo-Iranian people in south-east Anatolia, probably related to the ancient Medes. Their ethnic identity is denied by the Turks, and by 1990 there was a growing insurgency problem in the Kurdish area." (Draper, Edythe, ed. *The Almanac of the Christian World*, 1993-94 Edition. Wheaton, Il: Tyndale House, 1992, p. 144)

[28] "and in the seventh month, on the seventeenth day of the month, the ark came to rest on the mountains of Ararat" (Gen. 8:4 NRSV).

[29] "That very night the angel of the Lord set out and struck down one hundred eighty-five thousand in the camp of the Assyrians; when morning dawned, they were all dead bodies. Then King Sennacherib of Assyria left, went home, and lived at Nineveh. As he was worshiping in the house of his god Nisroch, his sons Adrammelech and Sharezer killed him with the sword, and they escaped into the land of Ararat. His son Esar-haddon succeeded him" (2 Kings 19:35-37 NRSV). Historical records place this event around 680 BC.

[30] Previously called Constantiople.

[31] In ancient times, Ankara was called Angora.

[32] The modern name is Selçuk or Efes.

⁣

33 Acts 18:19-24; Acts 19; Acts 20:16-38; Acts 21:29; 1 Corinthians 15:32; 1 Corinthians 16:8

34 1 Timothy 1:3; 2 Timothy 1:18; 4:12

36 Revelation 1:11; 2:1-7

36 Acts 18:18-21

37 Acts 19:10; 20:31

38 Estimated for 2000.

39 Estimated in 1998.

40 Estimated in 1997.

41 "Khalifat Rasul Allah" in Arabic.

42 Also called "Ramazan."

43 Also called "Seker Bayrami" in Turkey.

44 Also known as "Kurban Bayrami" in Turkey.

45 Sura 3:195

46 "The Prophet siad, 'I looked at Paradise and found poor people forming the majority of its inhabitants; and I looked at Hell and saw that the majoity of its inhabitants were women'" (Vol. 4, Book 54, No. 464: Imran bin Husain). "I heard the Prophet saying, 'Evil omen is in three things: the horse, the woman and the house'" (Vol. 4, Book 52, No. 110: Abdullah bin Umar).

47 Muslims believe Ishmael was Abraham's heir and their forefather rather than Isaac

48 Grilled meatballs and tomatoes on unleavened bread

49 www.bethany.com/profiles/clusters/8006.html

50 A Sufi brotherhood

51 Revelation 2-3 describes churches in the ancient cities of Ephesus, Smyrna, Pergamum, Thyatira, Sardis, Philadelphia, and Laodicea. Respectively, these are the modern cities of Efes, Izmir, Bergama, Akhisar, Salihli, Alasehir, and Denizli.

52 Johnstone, Patrick, Operation World. Grand Rapids, Michigan: Zondervan Publishing House, 1993, p. 541.

53 Turkey: A Time for Harvest. Littleton, Colorado: Caleb Project, 1997.

54 See note 52.

55 As told in a Turkish World Outreach Newsletter, 2000.

56 "Then I saw heaven opened, and there was a white horse! Its rider is called Faithful and True, and in righteousness he judges and makes war. His eyes are like a flame and he has a name inscribed that no one knows but himself. He is clothed in a robe dipped in blood, and his name is called The Word of God. And the armies of heaven, wearing fine linen, white and pure, were following him on white horses. From his mouth comes a sharp sword with which to strike down the nations, and he will rule them with a rod of iron; he will tread the winepress of the fury of the wrath of God the Almighty. On his robe and on his thigh he has a name inscribed, 'King of Kings and Lord of Lords'" (Rev. 19:11-16 NRSV).

57 Turkish World Outreach Newsletter, 2000. Names have not been given to protect those sharing their testimonies.

58 Ibid.

59 Ibid.

60 Doors of Opportunity: A Publication of First Baptist Church Woodstock, Georgia (1999).

61 Weston, David. "A New Thing." Doors of Opportunity: A Publication of First Baptist Church Woodstock, Georgia (1999).

62 Name has been changed to protect the person sharing.

63 Watson, Dwight G., "Beautiful but Dangerous: A Closer Look at Islam." Doors of Opportunity: A Publication of First Baptist Church Woodstock, Georgia (1999).

64 www.imb.org/imb/news/story.cfm?id=421

65 Ibid.

66 Ibid.

67 Watson, Dwight, "The Walking Warriors." Doors of Opportunity: A Publication of First Baptist Church Woodstock, Georgia (1999).

68 See Dispelling the Darkness in Turkey: Study Guide (W004120) for more information.

69 about 60 cents each

70 Replies from Turkey to Gospel Letter Volunteers, Turkish World Outreach. Names are not given to protect those quoted.

71 See note 60.

72 Hebrews 11:8

73 Exodus 4:1-16

74 Joshua 1:7

75 1 Samuel 3:8-9

76 Romans 1:1

Mission Study Evaluation

The 2000 International Mission Study for Adults consisted of a book (*Dispelling the Darkness in Turkey*) and a study guide. Your answers to this survey will help us create mission study products that meet your needs. Thank you for taking the time to fill out and return this evaluation form.

Please check the appropriate answer to each question below.

1. What role did you play in the adult international mission study?
_____ Teacher (a)   _____ Participant (b)

2. In my church's mission study:
_____ most people shared a study book (a)
_____ most people had their own study book (b)

3. How interesting was the mission study?
_____ (a) very interesting _____ (b) interesting _____ (c) boring

4. How informative was the mission study?
_____ (a) very informative _____ (b) informative _____ (c) not informative

5. How did you feel about the length of the study book?
_____ (a) good length _____ (b) too long _____ (c) too short

6. If you taught the study, how useful was the study guide?
_____ (a) useful _____ (b) adequate _____ (c) inadequate

7. If you taught the study, did you find enough activities to appropriately teach the material?
_____ (a) plenty of activities_____ (b) adequate number of activities
_____ (c) not enough activities

8. If you participated in or led the study, please answer the following by checking AGREE or DISAGREE. The 2000 International Mission Study . . .

AGREE   DISAGREE
_____ _____ . . . told me a lot about Islam.
_____ _____ . . . encouraged me to witness to Muslims in my area.
_____ _____ . . . left me with a desire to pray for Muslims in general.
_____ _____ . . . provided me with a useful plan to pray for Turks.
_____ _____ . . . encouraged me to volunteer in missions.
_____ _____ . . . gave me a desire to pray for missions and missionaries.
_____ _____ . . . increased my desire to give to missions.
_____ _____ . . . increased my knowledge of unreached people groups.
_____ _____ . . . left me open to serving God as a missionary.
_____ _____ . . . created in me a desire to know more about missions.

9. What did you like best about the study? What do you least? _____
_____

10. What was the most valuable insight you took away from the mission study? _____
_____

11. How could the next mission study be improved? _____
_____

Return evaluations to: Susan L. Hansen, Editor; Woman's Missionary Union;
100 Missionary Ridge; Birmingham, AL 35242